The Laws of Resilience

SEASON OF UNDERSTANDING

Praise for *The Laws of Resilience*

"To know Anthony is like reading a book you can't put down because every chapter ends with an unexpected moment that makes turning the page irresistible. Resilience isn't just measured by persevering through hardship; it's the condition of your heart when walking through extreme highs and lows. Culture dictates that our lives are ruled by fairness, and we live in response to our circumstances. Anthony taught me that when your destination has a higher purpose, expect the unexpected, and let your life pull you forward, not hold you back."

—Dr. Brian Russell, President, Iron House Coaching

"The old saying, 'You don't have a testimony without a trial' is true. *The Laws of Resilience* provide the reader, through Anthony's journey from adversity to triumph and his gift for teaching, a new framework for handling life's biggest challenges. I have walked alongside Anthony through some of his most transformative moments in the last few years, and as his close friend, I can attest that the authenticity and depth of his experience will give you a deep understanding of how to really engage life."

—The Honorable Vance D. Day, Former Circuit Court Judge

"Having known Anthony as a good & reliable friend, I can attest that *The Laws of Resilience* isn't just another self-help book—it's a masterclass in overcoming adversity from someone who has lived through extraordinary challenges and emerged even stronger as he authentically captures both his extraordinary gift for transforming lives, whether mentoring one person or electrifying an arena of thousands."

—**Nik Wallenda**, World-Renowned High-Wire Artist and Author

"*The Laws of Resilience* is a very practical yet powerful step-by-step guide to developing one of the most important assets in the human experience. Anthony does a great job of taking his own life experience and summarizing the lessons he's learned while  presenting them in such a way that illuminates, inspires, challenges, and equips you to grow in the midst of trials. I have had the privilege of doing life with Anthony as a close friend and brother. I have watched him up close and personal as he has endured the good, bad, and the ugly; and the wisdom in this book, make no mistake, if applied, will revolutionize your life, resulting in you being truly unbreakable!"

—**Burnard Scott Jr.**, Campus Pastor, Bayside Community Church

The Laws of Resilience

SEASON OF UNDERSTANDING

BY ANTHONY ROSARIO

Revenant
COACHING

Published by Revenant Coaching
an imprint of Revenant Enterprises, LLC
Bradenton, Florida
Email: consultations@revenantcoach.com

Interior Design by Imagine!® Studios
www.ArtsImagine.com

ISBN: 979-8-9928174-0-9 (paperback)
ISBN: 979-8-9928174-1-6 (e-book)

Library of Congress Control Number: 2025907145

First printing: August 2025

*"True resilience is not merely the capacity to endure,
but the strength to transform challenge into triumph."*

TABLE OF CONTENTS

Part One

KNOWING SELF

Part Two

KNOWING THE PATH

Part Three

KNOWING THE JOURNEY

Beginning the Journey

Dear Strength Seeker,

This is not just a book. It is an arsenal for life, a manual for those who refuse to be defeated. It is the first step in a transformative journey. This is Book One: "Season of Understanding" in The Laws of Resilience series. Why begin with understanding? Because true strength grows from deep roots. Before we can master resilience, we must first understand its nature, its elements, and its purpose. This season of understanding lays the foundation for all that will follow.

Every person will face moments of hardship, doubt, and loss. Some break under pressure. Others rise from the fire, stronger than before.

What makes the difference?

Resilience.

This book is the first in a four-part series designed to build your resilience step by step, through the four seasons of growth:

- **Season of Understanding (Book One)**—Building the foundation of resilience.
- **Season of Integration (Book Two)**—Uniting mind, body, and spirit.
- **Season of Application (Book Three)**—Applying resilience in real-world challenges.
- **Season of Mastery (Book Four)**—Achieving unshakable strength and wisdom.

We begin with understanding because strength without wisdom leads to recklessness. To master resilience, you must first know what it truly is.

By the end of this book, you will:

✔ Understand the foundations of resilience
✔ Identify your mental, physical, and spiritual strengths and weaknesses
✔ Develop a clear, actionable path forward

This is not an easy road. But those who walk it become unbreakable.

Welcome to the Laws of Resilience.

Your journey starts now.

ABOUT THE AUTHOR

 Anthony Rosario, known across America's corporate business networks and professional sports as "The Urban Legend," embodies the principles of resilience he teaches. As an Entrepreneur, Life Leader, Keynote Speaker, Author, Founder/President of A.R.M.S. Together, Founder/CEO of Revenant Coaching, and Founder/CEO of National Career Solutions—a recruiting firm connecting corporate giants and hungry professional talent with compatible precision—his impact reaches far beyond traditional boundaries of leadership development.

Born and raised in Chicago, Illinois, Anthony comes from proud family lineage shaped by a strong tradition of public service and law enforcement. His journey and message have reached some of the nation's most prestigious platforms, including Super Bowl LV (2021), where his story continues to inspire and transform lives.

What sets Anthony apart is not just his success, but the journey that forged it. His personal narrative—a uniquely powerful transformation from real-life nightmare to purpose-driven triumph—serves as living proof of the principles he teaches. This authentic experience forms the foundation of his unique and battle-tested leadership development initiatives.

As a motivating force, Anthony has dedicated his life to inspiring others through their personal struggles. His mission extends beyond mere motivation; it's about igniting hope and facilitating genuine restoration. Through his work, he demonstrates that true resilience isn't just about surviving challenges—it's about emerging stronger and using that strength to lift others.

Today, his impact continues to grow through A.R.M.S. Together and Revenant Coaching, where he helps individuals and organizations develop unshakeable resilience and authentic leadership capabilities. His approach combines hard-earned wisdom with practical strategies, delivering transformative results across all walks of life.

"My greatest achievement isn't in the platforms I've spoken on or the accolades I've received—it's in the lives transformed through the message of hope and resilience. Every challenge overcome becomes a bridge for others to cross."

—Anthony Rosario

The Foundation of Understanding

Before we build strength, we must understand its nature.

Imagine a warrior going into battle without knowing the terrain. He may have weapons, but if he does not understand the battlefield, he will fail.

Resilience works the same way. You must first know yourself, your path, and your journey before you can truly master it.

These are the **Three Pillars of Understanding**:

1. Knowing Self

- **Mind**: Your command center—where thoughts shape reality.
- **Body**: Your physical foundation—where strength meets endurance.
- **Spirit**: Your inner core—where purpose and resilience are forged.

2. Knowing the Path

- What resilience truly is (beyond just "bouncing back").
- How strength is cultivated (through challenges, not comfort).
- Why power must be guided by purpose (lest it becomes self-destructive).

3. Knowing the Journey

- **Where you begin**—Assessing your current state.
- **How you progress**—Recognizing the cycles of growth.
- **What lies ahead**—Understanding resilience as a lifelong pursuit.

Master these three pillars, and you will no longer just survive challenges—you will harness them as fuel for growth.

Part One
KNOWING SELF

CHAPTER 1

The Mind—Your First Teacher

The mind is your greatest weapon—or your greatest enemy. A weak mind leads to fear, hesitation, and failure. A strong mind creates clarity, resilience, and victory.

The Power of Thought

Your mind is a battlefield. Every victory or defeat begins here.

A person caught in a storm can see either:

1. A **disaster**—a force that threatens to destroy him/her.

2. An **opportunity**—a test that will make him stronger.

The event itself does not change. Only his perception does. And that perception determines whether he fights, flees, or adapts.

This is what separates the resilient from the defeated.

Recognizing Negative Thought Patterns

Your thoughts shape your reality. If you allow doubt, fear, and self-pity to dominate your mind, you will live in a world of limitations.

There are three destructive thought patterns that weaken resilience:

1. **The Victim Mindset**—"Why does this always happen to me?"
2. **The Fear-Based Mindset**—"What if I fail?"
3. **The Fixed Mindset**—"This is just the way I am."

Each of these is a trap. If you believe them, they become your reality.

But here is the truth:

Your thoughts are not absolute.

You can challenge, reframe, and reshape them.

Reframing Your Mindset: The Warrior's Lens

Instead of thinking, "I can't handle this," train your mind to ask, "How can I handle this?"

Instead of saying, "I'm not strong enough," tell yourself, "I am training to become stronger."

Instead of seeing failure as an ending, view it as a lesson.

This is The Warrior's Lens: A way of thinking that sees every obstacle as fuel for growth.

EXERCISE: Thought Pattern Awareness Journal

📝 **Goal**: Identify and reshape negative mental patterns.

⏳ **Duration:** 3 Days.

1. Each morning, write down three dominant thoughts in your mind.

2. Label them: Positive **(P),** Negative **(N),** or Neutral **(O)**.

3. At night, reflect: Which thoughts influenced your actions today?

4. Replace one negative thought with a more constructive reframe (e.g., *"I'm failing"* → *"I'm learning."*).

Next Steps: Building a Stronger Mind

✔ Understand your current thought patterns.

✔ Challenge every belief that weakens you.

✔ Reframe obstacles as opportunities.

✘ Master your mind, and you master your life.

CHAPTER 2

The Body–Your Physical Truth

Your body is not just a vessel—it is the foundation of your resilience.

A warrior cannot go into battle with a weak weapon. And yet, many people neglect the single most important weapon they have—their own body.

Your body is the vehicle through which mental and spiritual strength are expressed. It is not just flesh and bone—it is a high-performance machine that must be trained, maintained, and respected.

If you do not master your body, it will master you.

The Principles of Physical Resilience

Physical resilience is not just about brute strength or endurance—it is about understanding how to cultivate, protect, and optimize your body.

There are four principles that define physical resilience:

1. **Energy Management**—Knowing when to push hard and when to recover.

2. **Strength & Endurance**—Training not just for power, but for sustained performance.

3. **Physical Adaptability**—Building a body that can handle stress, pressure, and adversity.

4. **Longevity & Recovery**—Strength is useless if it burns out—true resilience is sustainable.

Each of these must be developed in balance—a body that is strong but exhausted is just as ineffective as one that is rested but weak.

Energy Management: Mastering Your Internal Battery

Your body runs on energy cycles, much like a high-performance engine. If you burn fuel too quickly without managing recovery, you will crash, weaken, and eventually break down.

Think of elite warriors or top athletes:

- They do not just train hard—they train smart.
- They strategically rest to allow maximum performance.
- They fuel their bodies properly so that every effort is optimized.

This is where most people fail. They either:

⚠ Overtrain and burn out

⚠ Undertrain and stay weak

⚠ Ignore their body's signals and suffer injury

The key to physical resilience is learning to read your body's signals and training in cycles:

- **Effort Phase:** Push hard, challenge limits.

9

- **Adaptation Phase:** Allow the body to strengthen and repair.

- **Sustainability Phase:** Maintain consistency without burnout.

If you master this rhythm, you will build a body that can endure, recover, and grow stronger over time.

EXERCISE: Tracking Energy Cycles

Goal: Identify and optimize your body's natural energy cycles.

Duration: 7 Days.

1. For one week, track your energy levels every 3 hours (Morning, Midday, Evening, Night).

2. Identify your peak and low energy times—when do you feel strongest? When do you feel weakest?

3. Track what affects your energy (food, sleep, stress, workouts).

4. Adjust one habit (e.g., better sleep, nutrition, hydration) and track changes.

Results: You will begin to understand how to optimize your body's natural energy for peak performance.

Strength & Endurance: Training for Battle

A strong body is not just aesthetically impressive—it is a shield against adversity.

The world will test you. Your body must be prepared.

The goal is not to train for appearance but for performance and resilience.

Principles of Functional Strength & Endurance:

✔ **Train for Functionality**—Your body must be able to move, lift, carry, and endure stress.

✔ **Develop Balanced Strength**—Train both muscle power and endurance for sustained performance.

✔ **Integrate Mental Toughness**—Every physical challenge is an opportunity to train the mind.

EXERCISE: Mental & Physical Endurance Test

Goal: Train both physical and mental resilience under controlled conditions.

Duration: 3 Days.

1. Choose a physical challenge slightly beyond your comfort zone (e.g., push-ups, running, lifting).

2. Set a target slightly higher than your normal limit.

3. Track your mental response: Do you quit early? Do you push through?

4. Repeat for 3 days, noticing how your mind adjusts to physical challenges.

Results: You will see that your body follows your mind—when you train the mind to push, the body follows.

Physical Adaptability: The True Test of Strength

Resilience is not just about lifting heavy or running far—it is about adapting to stress and pressure without breaking.

Imagine two warriors:

✗ **One is strong but rigid**—if he is thrown into an unfamiliar situation, he crumbles.

✗ **One is strong and adaptable**—he can fight in any environment, under any conditions.

Physical resilience is about building a body that adapts, not just one that endures.

This means:

✔ **Training under different conditions**—Heat, cold, fatigue, and pressure.

✔ **Building real-world movement**—Lifting, carrying, balancing, reacting.

✔ **Strengthening joints and tendons**—Preventing breakdown under strain.

EXERCISE: ADAPTABILITY CHALLENGE

📝 **Goal:** Test how well your body adapts to changing conditions.

⏳ **Duration:** 1 Week.

1. **Modify your workouts daily**—Change intensity, speed, environment, or stress levels.

2. **Challenge yourself to perform under fatigue**—Push one rep beyond comfort.

3. **Track your ability to adapt**—How does your body respond? Where do you struggle most?

Results: You will identify your weaknesses in adaptability and learn how to overcome them.

Longevity & Recovery: The Key to Sustainable Strength

A warrior who burns out early is no longer useful.

True resilience means staying strong for the long haul.

Recovery is not weakness—it is strategy.

Without proper recovery:

⚠️ You will break down.

⚠️ You will lose strength.

⚠️ You will fail when it matters most.

EXERCISE: Recovery Optimization

📝 **Goal:** Improve physical recovery for sustained resilience.

⏳ **Duration:** 7 Days.

1. Track your sleep, hydration, and muscle recovery each day.

2. Identify where you are neglecting recovery.

3. Implement one small change (stretching, hydration, sleep quality).

Results: You will feel stronger, recover faster, and sustain peak performance.

Final Thoughts: Become a Physical Warrior

✔ Train for function, endurance, and adaptability.

✔ Master energy cycles and recovery.

✔ Understand that physical resilience is a weapon—sharpen it.

Next, we will explore spiritual resilience—the anchor of true strength.

CHAPTER 3

The Spirit–Your Inner Guide

"At your center lies something deeper than
thought, more fundamental than the physical form.
It is the part of you that remains unbroken, even
when everything around you falls apart."

The Unbreakable Core

The mind commands your thoughts.

The body endures the physical battle.

But the spirit—your inner core—is what holds everything together when the storms of life come.

It is the anchor in adversity, the fuel of purpose, and the source of unshakable resilience.

Without it, a person may be strong in body, sharp in mind—but fragile in soul. And when the real tests come, they will crumble under pressure.

With it, you can face betrayal, loss, hardship, failure—and still rise again.

The Urban Legend: A Soul Forged in Fire

This is not just a theory. This is a truth that was lived.

There was a young man who was thrown into an abyss. His only weapons?

- A rock-sling in one hand.
- His heart in the other.

In his journal, he wrote:

"Into the abyss I shall go, broken in spirit—which no man shall ever know. Yet, a fearless soul they will see, for the stone I march into battle with is that of my heart."

For 4 years, he wandered through darkness, rebellion, and self-destruction.

- Misery was his companion.
- He feared no man—yet, he feared the silence.
- Because in the silence, he heard "the whispers of his King."

". . . This is not your end."

He fought. He conquered. He built a reputation in the abyss, feared by many. Yet in his journal, he wrote:

"Through resilience and strength in both knowledge and solidarity of HEART, I have become a feared mortal . . . loved by few, envied by many, and hated by the rest. But who have I become wherein now I even fear myself?"

Like every soul in that abyss, he too began to wear a mask to disguise his wounds, but his spirit was breaking.

Then, one night, the whispers of his King ultimately pierced his heart.

"Rise."

And so, he did.

For the next two decades, he fought not to survive—but to transform. He became a leader of multitudes. And when the time was right, his chains were unbound.

Today, his voice echoes from the highest mountains to the lowest valleys, declaring victory. His resilience became his greatest weapon.

✕ **This is the power of the spirit. The power of purpose. The power of transformation.**

And now, you must find yours.

What Is Spiritual Resilience?

Your spirit is not your emotions.

- **Emotions shift**—like the ocean's waves.
- **Your spirit is steady**—like the ocean floor.

If you build your resilience only on mental strength, it will crumble when emotions run wild.

If you build it only on physical endurance, it will fade when your body weakens.

But if you build it on something unshakable—your spirit, your purpose, your unbreakable core—nothing can destroy you.

The Three Pillars of Spiritual Resilience

To strengthen the spirit, you must cultivate three things:

1. **Inner Strength**—The ability to stand firm in your truth, no matter the storm.
2. **Purpose & Mission**—The deep reason that fuels you, beyond circumstances.
3. **Core Values**—The unshakable principles that guide your every action.

When these three pillars are strong, your resilience is indestructible.

Pillar One: Inner Strength

Inner strength does not mean hiding weakness—it means facing it and rising anyway.

- The bamboo bends in the storm—but does not break.
- The strongest warriors do not deny pain—they endure it and grow stronger.

True inner strength is not about being invulnerable—it's about being unbreakable despite vulnerability.

The Achilles Paradox

Even Achilles—the great warrior of legend—had one weakness.

But what made him powerful was not his invincibility—it was his unyielding spirit in the face of battle.

The truth is:

⚠️ You will have weaknesses.

⚠️ You will have doubts.

⚠️ You will face losses.

- But will you still stand?
- Will you still fight?

✗ That is inner strength.

EXERCISE: Building Your Inner Strength

📝 **Goal:** Identify and embrace your personal strength and weakness.

⏳ **Duration:** 20 Minutes.

1. Write down three personal strengths you rely on.

2. Write down one deep personal weakness that you fear.

3. Ask yourself: How has this weakness been shaping my decisions?

4. Write one actionable step to strengthen that weakness (ex: Fear of speaking? Join a public speaking group).

💡 **Lesson:** Strength is not the absence of weakness—it is learning how to face it and transform it.

Pillar Two: Purpose & Mission

When life becomes hard, your "reason why" must be greater than your excuse to quit.

Those who lack purpose break when the fire comes.

Those who have a deep, driving mission will push through anything.

- Why do you fight?
- Why do you refuse to quit?

- What is the mission that fuels you beyond yourself?

If you don't know the answers, you are walking through life without direction.

EXERCISE: Discovering Your Purpose

Goal: Define the mission that drives you.
Duration: 30 Minutes.

1. Write down five things you are deeply passionate about.

2. Write down three struggles you have overcome.

3. Ask yourself: What pain have I survived that I can now help others through?

4. Write one sentence that defines your mission in life.

Lesson: Your purpose is often found in the battles you have fought and won.

Pillar Three: Core Values

A warrior without a code is just another fighter.

A person without values will be tossed by every storm.

Your core values are the laws you live by, the principles you refuse to break, no matter the cost.

They are what keep you disciplined when no one is watching.

EXERCISE: Defining Your Core Values

📝 **Goal:** Solidify the unshakable principles that guide your life.

⏳ **Duration:** 20 Minutes.

1. Write down five values that define you.

2. Rank them from most important to least.

3. Reflect: Do my daily actions align with these values?

4. Choose one action that reinforces a key value this week.

💡 **Lesson:** A man's true strength is shown by what he refuses to compromise.

Final Thoughts: Become Unbreakable

✔ Build inner strength by facing your fears.

✔ Find your mission—let it fuel your resilience.

✔ Define your core values—live by them without compromise.

With these three pillars, your spirit becomes indestructible.

✕ **You will stand when others fall. You will rise when others break.**

Next, we will explore the true nature of resilience.
Are you ready?

Part Two

KNOWING THE PATH

CHAPTER 4

The Nature of Resilience

"Resilience is not just about enduring hardship.
It is about transforming hardship into power."

magine two warriors:

💀 **One stands in the fire but does not change**—he is hardened but brittle.

✕ **The other stands in the fire and transforms**—he is malleable yet unbreakable.

Which warrior will last longer?

The second, of course!

Resilience is not just about surviving pressure. It is about using that pressure to forge something stronger.

This chapter will teach you:

- What resilience truly is (beyond just "bouncing back").
- How resilience develops over time.
- Why resilience is the key to long-term strength.

Let's begin.

What Resilience Really Means

Most people think resilience means:

✗ "Pushing through no matter what."

✗ "Never breaking, never falling."

✗ "Being immune to failure and hardship."

That is false.

True resilience is the ability to:

✔ Fall but rise again—stronger.

✔ Endure pressure while transforming from it.

✔ Turn pain into power, setbacks into wisdom.

"The strongest steel is forged in the hottest fire."

Resilience is not about becoming indestructible—it is about becoming unbreakable through adaptability.

The Evolution of Resilience

Resilience is not something you are born with—it is something you develop through trial, struggle, and understanding.

It grows through three stages:

- **Stage 1: Survival Resilience**—Enduring hardship, pushing through.

- **Stage 2: Adaptive Resilience**—Learning to shift, evolve, and transform from challenge.

- **Stage 3: Mastered Resilience**—Harnessing every obstacle as fuel for greater power.

Let's break these down.

Stage 1: Survival Resilience

The first level of resilience is basic survival.

- You endure. You withstand. You push through.
- You refuse to quit, but you do not yet thrive.

Many people stay stuck here—they are strong, but their strength is rigid and exhausting.

They fight life instead of mastering it.

Stage 2: Adaptive Resilience

At this stage, you learn to use challenges as fuel.

- Instead of resisting change, you embrace it and grow from it.
- Instead of just enduring, you start transforming.

This is the moment you stop seeing struggles as setbacks and start seeing them as teachers.

"A river does not resist the rocks—it flows around them, shaping the landscape in its favor."

This is where true warriors separate from ordinary men.

Stage 3: Mastered Resilience

At this level, resilience is no longer something you "try" to have. It becomes who you are.

- **Obstacles excite you**—you see them as fuel for expansion.

- **You control your responses**, rather than reacting emotionally.

- **You do not fear hardship**—because you know it makes you stronger.

This is where masters live.

✗ Resilience is no longer about surviving or adapting—it is about thriving no matter the conditions.

EXERCISE: Identifying Your Level of Resilience

📝 **Goal:** Determine where you are in your resilience journey.

⏳ **Duration:** 15 Minutes.

1. Write down a recent hardship or challenge you faced.

2. Reflect: How did you handle it?

   - Did you just endure it? (*Survival Resilience*)

- Did you learn from it and grow? (*Adaptive Resilience*)

- Did you use it as fuel to elevate yourself? (*Mastered Resilience*)

3. Record one way to push yourself to the next level.

💡 **Lesson:** The goal is not just to "survive" life's tests, but to master them.

Where Resilience Leads

Resilience is not just about personal toughness. It is about where it takes you.

There are three destinations that resilience creates:

✔ **Personal Strength**—You become unshakable, no matter the storm.

✔ **Emotional Control**—You dictate your reactions, rather than being ruled by them.

✔ **True Freedom**—You are no longer controlled by fear, failure, or external circumstances.

Most people are slaves to their emotions, their past, or their limitations. But a resilient person? They are free.

"Resilience is not just about enduring pain. It is about transforming pain into power."

You are now on that path.

Final Thoughts: Transitioning to True Strength

✔ Understand that resilience is about growth, not just endurance.

✔ Recognize where you are in your resilience journey.

✔ Commit to rising above survival—toward mastery.

In the next chapter, we will explore the deeper elements of strength—how it is built, how it integrates, and how to wield it properly.

You have learned what resilience is. Now, it is time to make it part of your identity.

CHAPTER 5

The Elements of Strength

"True strength is not just about power—it is about knowing when to use it, when to withhold it, and how to integrate it into every aspect of your life."

A warrior does not become great by merely lifting a sword— he becomes great when he masters the balance between strength, control, and purpose.

Most people believe strength is about brute force—about being the most powerful, the most dominant.

But in truth, real strength is about integration.

- A person can be physically powerful but emotionally weak.
- A person can be mentally sharp but spiritually lost.

- A person can be driven by willpower but easily broken by failure.

Strength is not found in just one element. It is the union of all elements—mind, body, and spirit—that creates unshakable resilience.

The Four Elements of True Strength

Strength is not one-dimensional—it is a system.

To be truly strong, you must develop all four elements of strength:

1. **Mental Strength**—Clarity, discipline, and the ability to control thoughts.

2. **Physical Strength**—Power, endurance, and the ability to withstand pressure.

3. **Emotional Strength**—Mastery of reactions, resilience under stress.

4. **Spiritual Strength**—Purpose, moral conviction, and an unbreakable core.

✕ **When these four forces work together, strength is no longer just something you "have"—it becomes who you are.**

Let's break them down.

1. Mental Strength: The Command Center

"Your mind is your strongest weapon—
if you learn to wield it."

A person with a strong body but a weak mind will crumble under pressure.

A person who lacks discipline, clarity, or focus will never sustain real strength.

The Three Core Skills of Mental Strength:

✔ **Clarity Under Pressure**—The ability to think clearly even in chaos.

✔ **Unshakable Focus**—Training your mind to cut through distractions.

✔ **Mental Toughness**—Strengthening your mind against doubt, fear, and uncertainty.

✕ **Mental strength is about controlling your inner world so that nothing external can shake you.**

EXERCISE: Strengthening Your Mental Discipline

📝 **Goal:** Train your mind to handle pressure with clarity.

⏳ **Duration:** 7 Days.

1. Each morning, write down one thing that could mentally throw you off today.

2. Identify how you will choose to respond instead of reacting emotionally.

3. At the end of the day, reflect: Did you stay in control?

4. Repeat daily, tracking your progress.

💡 **Lesson:** You are not controlled by your thoughts or emotions—you command them.

2. Physical Strength: The Foundation of Power

"Your body is not just a tool—it is your fortress."

A strong body supports a strong mind. When you train your body to push past limits, your mind follows.

The Three Core Aspects of Physical Strength:

✔ **Endurance**—The ability to sustain effort over time.

✔ **Power**—The ability to exert force when necessary.

✔ **Control**—The ability to move efficiently without wasted energy.

✗ **Physical strength is not just about muscle—it's about discipline, movement, and control.**

EXERCISE: Pushing Your Physical Limits

📝 **Goal:** Identify where you can push your body further.
⏳ **Duration:** 7 Days.

1. Choose one physical challenge slightly beyond your current level (running, lifting, endurance).

2. Commit to pushing just 5% further than usual.

3. Observe how your mind reacts to fatigue—does it tell you to quit, or can you push further?

4. Track improvements over a week.

💡 **Lesson:** Your body follows your mind—train one, and the other strengthens.

3. Emotional Strength: Mastering Your Reactions

"A person who cannot control their emotions is a person who can be controlled by anyone."

Most people are slaves to their emotions.

- If they feel anger, they lash out.
- If they feel doubt, they quit.
- If they feel fear, they hesitate.

A man with emotional strength does not react impulsively—he responds with mastery.

The Three Core Aspects of Emotional Strength:

✔ **Emotional Control**—The ability to respond instead of react.

✔ **Resilience Under Stress**—Withstanding emotional pressure without breaking.

✔ **Emotional Intelligence**—Understanding your own emotions and those of others.

✘ **True emotional strength means you are not easily provoked, broken, or shaken.**

EXERCISE: Testing Your Emotional Control

📝 **Goal:** Identify and strengthen your weakest emotional response.

⏳ **Duration:** 3 Days.

1. Identify one emotion that often controls you (anger, frustration, doubt, fear).

2. Each time it arises, pause and assess it rather than reacting.

3. Choose a new, controlled response instead of the automatic one.

4. Track moments where you successfully controlled your emotional state.

💡 **Lesson:** If you control your emotions, you cannot be manipulated, weakened, or broken.

4. Spiritual Strength: The Unbreakable Core

"A person without purpose is easily destroyed. A person with purpose can withstand anything."

A person who lacks a deep "why" will collapse under pressure.

A person with a clear mission, an unshakable belief, and a strong inner compass will push through anything.

The Three Core Aspects of Spiritual Strength:

✔ **A Deep Sense of Purpose**—Knowing what you stand for.

✔ **Moral Conviction**—Living by an unshakable code.

✔ **Inner Peace**—Remaining stable no matter what happens around you.

✗ Spiritual strength is what gives all other strength direction and endurance.

EXERCISE: Discovering Your Deep "Why"

📝 **Goal:** Identify and strengthen your life's purpose.

⏳ **Duration:** 30 Minutes.

1. Write down three struggles you have overcome.

2. Ask yourself: How can these struggles shape my purpose?

3. Write a one-sentence mission statement that defines your deeper "why".

4. Reflect: Are my daily actions aligned with this mission?

💡 **Lesson:** A strong man does not wander—he moves with purpose.

Final Thoughts: The Power of Integration

✔ Mental strength gives you control over thoughts.

✔ Physical strength gives you power and endurance.

✔ Emotional strength gives you control over reactions.

✔ Spiritual strength gives you an unbreakable purpose.

When these four forces are mastered together, you do not just become strong—you become a force of nature.

In the next chapter, we will explore the purpose of power—why we seek strength, how to use it wisely, and where it leads.

✗ **It is not enough to be strong. You must learn how to wield that strength with wisdom.**

CHAPTER 6

The Purpose of Power

"Power without purpose is like a sword without a hilt—
it cuts the wielder as much as it cuts the enemy."

M any people seek power—whether it is physical strength, influence, or success.

But power without purpose is dangerous.

- A person with power but no discipline becomes reckless.
- A person with strength but no control becomes a brute.
- A person with success but no mission becomes empty.

This chapter will teach you:

✔ Why we seek power.
✔ How to use power wisely.

✔ Where power leads—and how it can shape or destroy you.

Why We Seek Strength

Power is not inherently good or bad. It is simply a tool.

- Some seek power to control.
- Some seek power to protect.
- Some seek power to build.

The question is not whether you have power—but what you will do with it.

> *"The highest form of power is not in*
> *destruction—but in creation."*

✕ To wield power correctly, we must understand its purpose.

The Three Levels of Power

Power exists in three levels:

1. **Power Over Self**—The foundation: mastery of mind, body, and emotions.

2. **Power Over Circumstances**—The ability to shape and influence the external world.

3. **Power Over Others**—Leadership, responsibility, and the weight of influence.

A weak man seeks only the third level—to dominate others without first mastering himself.

A strong man masters himself first, then his world, then leads others with wisdom.

1. Power over Self: The First Battle

"A person who cannot command themself
is not fit to command others."

Before you seek to influence the world, you must first control your own actions, thoughts, and desires.

- Can you keep a promise to yourself?
- Can you discipline your mind when it wants to quit?

- Can you control your emotions rather than let them control you?

If not, you are a prisoner of your own impulses.

⚔ **Self-mastery is the first level of true power. Without it, all other power is unstable.**

EXERCISE: Testing Self-Mastery

📝 **Goal:** Strengthen your ability to control your own actions.

⏳ **Duration:** 3 Days.

1. Choose one small but difficult discipline to commit to (waking up early, cold showers, 30 minutes of reading, etc.).

2. Do it consistently for three days, no excuses.

3. Each day, reflect: How does your mind react? What excuses arise? Do you push through?

💡 **Lesson:** Mastering yourself is harder than mastering others—but once you do, you become unstoppable.

2. Power over Circumstances: Shaping Your World

Once you have control over yourself, you gain control over your environment.

- You no longer react to life—you dictate how life reacts to you.
- You stop making excuses—you take responsibility.
- You stop waiting—you create opportunities.

This is where a strong person separates from a weak person.

A weak person blames their job, their past, their circumstances.

A strong person takes what he/she has and makes something of it.

EXERCISE: Taking Control of Your Circumstances

📝 **Goal:** Identify and take action in an area where you feel powerless.

⏳ **Duration:** 1 Hour.

1. Write down one area where you feel stuck or powerless.

2. Identify what is within your control (actions, mindset, strategies).

3. Take one immediate action to reclaim control.

💡 **Lesson:** Power over your environment starts when you stop waiting and start acting.

3. Power over Others: The Burden of Leadership

Real power is not about control—it is about responsibility.

The moment you have influence—whether over family, a team, or a business—you carry a weight.

- Weak men misuse power to dominate.
- Strong men use power to protect, guide, and build.

If your power only serves yourself, it is corrupt.
If your power uplifts others, it is honorable.

> *"The highest warriors are not those who conquer men—but those who conquer themselves and inspire others to do the same."*

EXERCISE: Defining Your Leadership Principles

📝 **Goal:** Clarify how you will use your power and influence.

⏳ **Duration:** 20 Minutes.

1. Write down three key principles that will guide how you use power.

2. Reflect: Have you ever used power (your words, influence, or authority) in a way that harmed or helped?

3. Write one commitment to use power responsibly in the future.

💡 **Lesson:** The strongest men are not those who take power—but those who use it wisely.

Where Power Leads: The Two Paths

Power will always lead you to one of two places:

💀 **The Path of Destruction**—If you let power consume you, it will break you.

✕ **The Path of Purpose**—If you use power wisely, it will elevate you and those around you.

The Corrupt Path

💀 Power used for ego, dominance, or greed leads to downfall.

💀 It blinds you, makes you reckless, and isolates you.

💀 History is filled with great men who fell because they let power consume them.

The Noble Path

✔ Power used for protection, service, and wisdom leads to legacy.

✔ It strengthens your spirit rather than corrupts it.

✔ The greatest warriors are those who mastered the balance between power and restraint.

✗ **The highest form of power is not control, but wisdom.**

Final Thoughts: Mastering the Purpose of Power

✔ Power begins with self-mastery.

✔ Power extends to shaping your world.

✔ Power reaches its highest form when used for service, not ego.

It is not enough to be strong—you must know how to wield your strength with wisdom.

In the next chapter, we will explore the journey of resilience—where it starts, how it progresses, and what lies ahead.

✗ **True power is not about dominance. It is about purpose.**

Are you ready to step into yours?

Part Three
KNOWING THE JOURNEY

CHAPTER 7

The Starting Point

"A warrior does not set out on a journey without first understanding his position on the map."

Most people fail in their journey of resilience not because they lack strength, but because they lack direction. They move blindly, without assessing:

- Where they are now.
- What tools they have at their disposal.
- What obstacles they must prepare for.

Before you can advance, you must face your reality with absolute clarity.

This chapter will guide you to:

✔ Take an honest inventory of your current state.

✔ Identify your strengths, weaknesses, and resources.

✔ Map out the challenges you must overcome.

✔ See your full potential—and take the first step toward it.

The Three Questions of Self-Assessment

Every warrior asks himself three critical questions before setting out on a mission:

1. **Where am I now?** (Assessing your current state)
2. **What do I have?** (Recognizing your strengths and resources)
3. **What stands in my way?** (Identifying obstacles and weaknesses)

By answering these questions with full honesty, you gain control over your path forward.

Question 1: Where Am I Now?

Most people avoid this question because they fear the answer.

They don't want to face the reality of:

- How weak they have allowed themselves to become.
- How many excuses they have made.
- How much they have avoided responsibility.

But a warrior faces reality head-on.

Before you grow, you must assess your current position without excuses, without lies, without self-pity.

✕ **The truth will not weaken you—it will set you free.**

EXERCISE: Self-Assessment Inventory

📝 **Goal:** Get a clear picture of where you currently stand.

⏳ **Duration:** 30 Minutes.

1. Write down three areas where you feel strong.

2. Write down three areas where you feel weak.

3. Ask yourself: Are my weaknesses due to lack of skill, lack of discipline, or fear?

4. Reflect: What is the hardest truth I must admit about myself right now?

💡 **Lesson:** Strength begins with brutal honesty. The more clearly you see yourself, the stronger you can become.

Question 2: What Do I Have?

Many people focus only on what they lack, never realizing how many resources and strengths they already possess.

- You have skills and knowledge you've built over time.
- You have relationships and mentors who can guide you.
- You have resilience from past battles you've already survived.

Even in your weakest moments, you are not empty-handed.

✕ *"A warrior who knows his weapons can fight, even when outnumbered."*

EXERCISE: Identifying Your Resources

📝 **Goal:** Recognize the strengths and tools you already have.

⏳ **Duration:** 15 Minutes.

1. Write down three skills or strengths you already possess.

2. Write down three past struggles you survived—what did they teach you?

3. Write down three people in your life who challenge or support you.

💡 **Lesson:** No matter how difficult life seems, you already have weapons for the battle ahead.

Question 3: What Stands in My Way?

Every warrior must assess his enemies and obstacles before stepping into battle.

There are three major types of obstacles:

1. External Obstacles (Life's Challenges)

These are the things outside of your control—financial struggles, family issues, job stress.

You cannot control them, but you can control your response to them.

2. Internal Obstacles (Your Weaknesses)

These are the flaws inside you—laziness, doubt, fear, lack of discipline.

These are the true enemies, because they are the ones that hold you back the most.

3. Mental Obstacles (False Beliefs & Excuses)

These are the stories you tell yourself about why you "can't" move forward.

- "I'm too old."
- "It's too late."
- "I don't have enough experience."
- "I wasn't born with natural talent."

🏴 These are lies. If you let them control you, you will never grow.

⚔ *"A weak mind builds excuses. A strong mind breaks through them."*

EXERCISE: Destroying Obstacles

📝 **Goal:** Identify and dismantle the things holding you back.

⏳ **Duration:** 30 Minutes.

1. Write down one external challenge you currently face.

   - Identify: What is within your control?

2. Write down one internal weakness (laziness, fear, doubt, etc.).

   - Identify: What is one small way to weaken its control over you?

3. Write down one limiting belief you've told yourself.

   - Identify: What is the truth that destroys this belief?

💡 **Lesson:** Your greatest enemies are not outside of you—they are inside your mind.

Seeing Your Full Potential

Now that you have assessed:

✔ Where you are.
✔ What strengths and resources you have.
✔ What obstacles stand in your way.

It is time to face your potential.

Many men see only their current limitations—not realizing how powerful they can become.

The Future You Already Exists

There is a stronger version of you already out there.

- He is more disciplined than you are today.
- He is more resilient than you are today.
- He has mastered his weaknesses that still control you.

The only thing separating you from him is the work you put in every single day.

EXERCISE: Meeting Your Future Self

Goal: Envision the strongest version of yourself.

Duration: 15 Minutes.

1. Close your eyes and picture yourself five years from now, having reached your full potential.

2. Write down what this version of you looks like, acts like, and thinks like.

3. Write down what habits and disciplines this version of you has.

4. Identify one step you can take today to move toward that future version of yourself.

Lesson: The stronger version of you already exists—your job is to catch up to him.

Final Thoughts: Building a Strong Foundation

✔ You now know where you stand.

✔ You have identified your strengths and weaknesses.

✔ You have mapped out your obstacles.

✔ You have seen the path to your full potential.

This is your starting point.

In the next chapter, we will explore how to progress along this path—how to grow, adapt, and transform over time.

You now have clarity. The only thing left is action. Are you ready?

CHAPTER 8

The Path of Progress

"Progress is not a straight road. It is a
battlefield with victories, setbacks, and lessons.
The key is to keep moving forward."

The Truth About Progress

M ost people believe true growth simply happens like this:

- Work hard.
- See improvement.
- Keep advancing steadily.

But this is a myth.

In reality, progress looks more like this:

✔ Struggle in the beginning.

✔ Make initial progress.

✔ Hit unexpected obstacles.

✔ Feel stuck in a plateau.

✔ Break through with persistence.

✔ Grow stronger, only to face new challenges.

This is how resilience develops.

Growth is not linear—it is cyclical, much like the seasons of nature.

The Three Phases of Growth

Resilience and personal transformation happen in three distinct phases:

- **Phase 1: Recognition**—Understanding what must change.
- **Phase 2: Development**—Building new habits, discipline, and strength.
- **Phase 3: Mastery**—Fully embodying resilience as part of your identity.

Let's break these down.

Phase 1: Recognition—Seeing the Truth

"You cannot change what you refuse to see."

Before you grow, you must first recognize what needs to change.

This means:

- Facing your weaknesses without denial.
- Identifying your excuses without self-pity.
- Admitting where you fall short—not as failure, but as fuel for growth.

✕ **Recognition is painful. But without it, there is no progress.**

EXERCISE: Identifying Your Growth Points

📝 **Goal:** Pinpoint the exact areas where you need to improve.

⏳ **Duration:** 20 Minutes.

1. Write down one area in your life where you feel weak or undisciplined.

2. Identify why this area has remained weak—what excuses or fears have held you back?

3. Write one small but immediate action you can take to improve this area today.

💡 **Lesson:** Strength begins with recognizing where you are weak—and committing to change.

Phase 2: Development—The Hard Work Begins

"Once you see the path, you must walk it."

This is the grind phase—the part where you do the work, even when it's hard, slow, and frustrating.

Most people quit here because:

❌ Progress is slower than they expected.

❌ They hit obstacles and think they are failing.

❌ The excitement fades, and discipline is required.

❌ **This is where warriors are forged.**

Progress in this phase is about consistency, not speed.

You may not feel like you're improving, but every rep, every small action, every battle won against your old self is making you stronger.

How to Sustain Momentum

To survive this phase, you must:

✔ **Commit to the process**—even when it feels slow.

✔ **Track small wins**—so you don't lose motivation.

✔ **Push through plateaus**—by making small but intentional improvements.

The secret to long-term growth is not intensity—it is consistency.

EXERCISE: Building Daily Discipline

📝 **Goal:** Develop unstoppable momentum through small, consistent actions.

⏳ **Duration:** 7 Days.

1. Choose one habit that aligns with your resilience journey (working out, reading, journaling, meditating).

2. Commit to doing it for 7 straight days—no excuses.

3. Track your success each day.

4. If you miss a day, immediately restart without guilt.

💡 **Lesson:** The warrior's path is about showing up every day, no matter how small the step.

Phase 3: Mastery—Becoming the Warrior

"At first, discipline is something you force.
But over time, it becomes who you are."

Mastery happens when:

- You no longer have to force resilience—it becomes automatic.
- You handle adversity without panic or hesitation.
- You are so consistent in your habits that they define your identity.

At this stage, resilience is no longer something you "try" to have. It is part of you.

Signs You Are Reaching Mastery

✗ You no longer feel resistance to hard work—you embrace it.

✗ You recover quickly from failure—you see setbacks as feedback.

✗ You lead others by example—because resilience radiates from you.

This is when you truly own your strength.

"The master has failed more times than the beginner has even tried."

EXERCISE: Defining Your Future Self

📝 **Goal:** Step into the identity of the strongest version of yourself.

⏳ **Duration:** 20 Minutes.

1. Write down a vision statement of who you are becoming.

   - Example: *"I am a **man / woman** of resilience, discipline, and strength. I face every challenge head-on. I do not quit. I do not break. I move with purpose."*

2. Identify three habits you must master to become this person.

3. Start acting like that person today.

💡 **Lesson:** Your future self is not someone you become—it is someone you decide to be, every single day.

How to Overcome Plateaus

At some point, you will feel stuck—like you are making no progress.

When this happens:

✔️ **Change your strategy**—introduce new challenges.

✔️ **Go back to fundamentals**—simplify your approach.

✔️ **Seek mentorship**—learn from those ahead of you.

"If you feel stuck, you are not failing. You are at the edge of your next breakthrough."

Final Thoughts: Staying On the Path

✔ Recognize where you need to grow.

✔ Commit to daily progress—no matter how small.

✔ Embrace plateaus as part of the journey.

✔ Step into mastery—where resilience becomes part of your identity.

✗ **The path of resilience is never-ending. But those who stay on it become unstoppable.**

In the next chapter, we will explore what lies ahead—the long-term vision, the greater journey, and the legacy you will leave behind.

Are you ready to see what's beyond the horizon?

CHAPTER 9

The Vision Ahead

"A warrior does not fight only for today—
he fights for the future he is building."

U p until now, we have focused on understanding resilience,
building strength, and mastering progress.

But resilience is not just about surviving today's battles—it
is about creating a future worth fighting for.

This chapter will help you:

✔ See the bigger picture—your long-term journey.
✔ Understand the seasons of resilience—how growth
evolves over time.
✔ Clarify your purpose—why you are fighting in the first
place.

✔ Step into the role of a leader—building a legacy beyond yourself.

This is where everything comes together.

The Greater Journey of Resilience

Most people only think one step ahead.
They ask:

- "How do I get through today?"
- "How do I handle this problem?"
- "How do I survive this season of life?"

But warriors think beyond the immediate battle.
They ask:

✔ "Where is this leading me?"

✔ "How does this moment shape my long-term growth?"

✔ "What kind of person am I becoming?"

If you only focus on the next fight, you will always be reacting to life.

If you focus on the long-term vision, you will start shaping life on your own terms.

✕ "A great warrior does not train just for one battle—he trains for the entire war."

This is how you build a future of strength, purpose, and legacy.

The Seasons of Resilience

Just like nature moves through seasons, your personal growth follows cycles.

Every warrior must pass through four key seasons in his journey:

- **Season 1: Understanding**—Laying the foundation, discovering resilience.

- **Season 2: Integration**—Unifying mind, body, and spirit into a cohesive force.

- **Season 3: Application**—Testing resilience in the real world through challenges.

- **Season 4: Mastery**—Achieving unshakable strength and guiding others.

Each season builds on the last.

Most people never make it past Season 1—they gain knowledge, but never integrate it.

Your goal is to move through every season, reaching true mastery.

Which Season Are You In?

- **Season 1 (Understanding)**—You are learning about resilience, breaking old patterns.

- **Season 2 (Integration)**—You are applying discipline, consistency, and mental toughness

- **Season 3 (Application)**—You are testing your strength in real-world challenges.

- **Season 4 (Mastery)**—Resilience is now part of you; you lead and inspire others.

Most people get stuck in learning. Warriors move to application and mastery.

EXERCISE: Identifying Your Season

📝 **Goal:** Determine where you are in your resilience journey.

⌛ **Duration:** 15 Minutes.

1. Ask yourself: Am I still learning, or am I applying?

2. Write down which season you are in and why.

3. Identify one action to move to the next level.

💡 **Lesson:** Growth is not about time—it is about action. What you do today determines how fast you progress.

Seeing Your Long-Term Purpose

If you fight without a deeper purpose, you will eventually burn out.

- A warrior does not fight just to fight.
- A warrior fights for something greater than himself.

Your purpose is your North Star—it keeps you on course, even in the darkest storms.

✗ **"A person with a purpose is unstoppable. A person without one is already defeated."**

EXERCISE: Clarifying Your Purpose

Goal: Define the deeper mission that drives you.

Duration: 30 Minutes.

1. Write down three things that deeply matter to you.

2. Identify a challenge you have overcome—how can you use it to help others?

3. Write a purpose statement:

- *"I am committed to [action] because [reason] in order to [impact]."*
- Example: *"I am committed to self-mastery because I refuse to be weak, in order to lead and inspire others."*

💡 **Lesson:** When your purpose is clear, your motivation never runs out.

Becoming a Leader & Building a Legacy

The final stage of resilience is not just about personal strength—it is about becoming a leader and leaving an impact.

A true warrior does not just:

✔ Train himself.

✔ Overcome his own obstacles.

✔ Achieve personal success.

A true warrior also:

- Lifts others up.
- Leads by example.
- Leaves a legacy that lasts beyond his lifetime.

✗ "The strongest warriors are those who fight not just for themselves, but for those who come after them."

EXERCISE: Defining Your Legacy

Goal: Identify the impact you want to leave behind.

Duration: 20 Minutes.

1. Imagine yourself 20 years in the future—what do you want to be remembered for?

2. Write down how your actions today are shaping that legacy.

3. Identify one way to start leading and impacting others right now.

💡 **Lesson:** Strength is meaningless if it dies with you. True power is passing on what you have built.

Food for Thought– Preparing for Season Two

✔ You now see the long-term vision.

✔ You understand that growth happens in seasons.

✔ You have defined your deeper purpose.

✔ You are stepping into leadership and legacy.

Now, you are ready for the next phase: Integration.

You have built the foundation. Now, it is time to forge it into something unbreakable.

EXERCISE: Committing to Action

📝 **Goal:** Solidify your commitment to growth beyond this book.

⌛ **Duration:** 20 Minutes.

1. Write down three key lessons you have learned from this book.

2. Write down three specific actions you will take in the next 30 days.

3. Sign this commitment:

   "I commit to applying what I have learned. I will take action. I will not make excuses. I will become stronger—mentally, physically, and spiritually. This is not just a decision. This is my path."

💡 **Lesson:** The only difference between those who grow and those who stay the same is who takes action.

   Will you?

The Journey Continues

- You have built your foundation.
- You have seen the path ahead.
- You now know what must be done.

Now, you must walk the path.

This book was the first step. The next steps will be more challenging, more intense—but also more transformative.

⚠️ Many people finish books and change nothing.

✕ You will be different.

Because true warriors do not just seek knowledge—they live it.

✕ "The battle is not won in a single day. It is won in the choices made every day."

Final Chapter Extension: The Legacy You Forge

"Resilience does not end when the battle is won. It begins when the victory turns into a bridge for others to cross."

You have arrived at the culmination of the Season of Understanding. But just as the setting sun does not signify the end of light, this chapter is not an ending—it is an awakening.

This is where resilience takes its highest form: not merely as a tool for personal survival, but as a catalyst for something greater. The journey you've undertaken thus far has strengthened your mind, body, and spirit, but now you must ask yourself a deeper question:

What will you do with this strength?

Will it remain a private victory, or will it serve as a guiding light for others?

This chapter is about the transition from self-mastery to service. It is about understanding that resilience is not meant to stop with you—it is meant to flow through you, creating ripples that extend beyond your life.

The Shift from Warrior to Builder

"A warrior fights for survival. A builder fights for creation."

Until now, your focus has been on developing personal resilience:

✔ Reframing negative thoughts.
✔ Strengthening your body and endurance.
✔ Awakening your spirit through purpose and conviction.

This focus was necessary. But the time has come to shift your role. You are no longer just a warrior fighting internal battles—you are a builder tasked with creating something that endures.

What do warriors-turned-builders create?

1. **Legacies of Impact**: Actions that inspire, transform, and empower others.

2. **Structures of Guidance**: Principles and teachings that remain long after you are gone.

3. **Foundations of Strength**: A life that shows others what is possible when resilience becomes a way of being.

This shift is not about abandoning the battles—it is about fighting with a higher purpose.

The Three Laws of Legacy

If resilience is the sword you have sharpened, legacy is the cause you fight for. But legacy is not built randomly—it follows its own set of rules.

Law 1: Legacy Requires Purpose Beyond Yourself

Personal resilience begins with the self, but legacy is built when you channel your strength into something greater. Ask yourself:

- Who benefits from your growth?
- What causes or communities can you uplift with what you've learned?
- How can your journey inspire those still struggling in the darkness?

✗ *Purpose is the bridge between personal strength and lasting impact.*

Without purpose, resilience becomes self-contained. But when guided by a cause, it becomes a source of transformation for others.

Exercise: Write down three ways your current strengths can be used to uplift or inspire someone else.

Law 2: Legacy is Built Daily, Not in a Single Act

Many think legacy is about grand achievements—becoming famous, building empires, or leaving behind monumental creations. But true legacy is built in the small, consistent decisions you make every day.

✔ How you treat others.

✔ How you honor your commitments.

✔ How you respond when life challenges you.

It's in these daily choices that you write the story of your life.

✗ *Consistency, not greatness, creates lasting impact.*

The people who will remember you won't necessarily recall your biggest victories. They will remember the quiet strength you showed when things were hard, the guidance you offered when they were lost, and the lessons you left behind in how you lived.

Law 3: Legacy Outlives You When You Share It

Resilience that dies with you is wasted potential.

To create a lasting legacy, you must pass on what you've learned:

- Teach someone the lessons you wish you had known sooner.
- Lead by example, showing others how to rise from failure.
- Document your journey through writing, storytelling, or mentorship.

✗ *A person who shares their wisdom is a person whose legacy will never die.*

The Mark You Leave: A Reflection Exercise

📝 **Goal:** Reflect on the kind of legacy you want to leave.
⏳ **Duration:** 15 Minutes.

1. Imagine your future self 20 years from now. What impact do you hope to have made on others?

2. Write down three lessons you want to be remembered for.

3. Identify one person or community you can help today using what you have learned.

💡 **Reminder:** You don't need to wait until you've mastered everything to make an impact. Even now, someone can benefit from what you've overcome.

Becoming a Mentor of Resilience

The greatest warriors do not seek to conquer—they seek to guide. There is someone right now—perhaps a friend, a sibling, a colleague, or a stranger—who is fighting a battle you've already overcome. Your guidance could be the difference between their defeat and their victory.

Ways to Lead by Example:

✔ **Share Your Story:** Vulnerability is not weakness—it is power. Let others see that even warriors struggle before they rise.

✔ **Offer Support Without Judgment:** Help others grow without expecting perfection. Guide them as someone who knows the difficulty of the journey.

✔ **Challenge Others to Grow:** True leaders do not comfort people into stagnation—they push them toward their potential.

The Legacy You Begin Now

Legacy is not something you leave behind after death—it is something you create while you are alive. Every action you take today contributes to it.

- When you choose discipline over laziness, you build a legacy of resilience.
- When you show compassion instead of indifference, you build a legacy of empathy.
- When you overcome fear and take action, you build a legacy of courage.

Legacy is not built by extraordinary people. It is built by ordinary people who make extraordinary decisions every day.

A Final Message from the Author

"I began this journey thinking that resilience was something I needed to survive. But I learned that resilience is the key to living fully, unapologetically, and with purpose. I didn't just survive—I became someone who could thrive in any storm and show others how to do the same. That is the real reward: not just transforming yourself, but transforming the world around you."

Now, it's your turn.

FINAL EXERCISE: Planting Seeds of Legacy

Goal: Commit to one action that will contribute to your legacy.

Duration: 20 Minutes.

1. Write down one lesson from your journey that you want to pass on to others.

2. Identify one person or group who could benefit from this lesson.

3. Take one action this week to share it. This could be a conversation, a letter, or an act of mentorship.

> 💡 **Remember:** Legacy is not about recognition—it's about the impact you make, even if no one sees it.

Walking Into Season Two with Purpose

As you close the Season of Understanding, understand this: you have not just learned resilience—you have become it. The challenges that once intimidated you now look like opportunities for growth. The doubts that once held you back now serve as fuel for progress.

But the greatest victory is yet to come.

Season Two will challenge you to integrate all of this knowledge into action. It will test whether you can stay disciplined when life becomes chaotic, whether you can lead others without losing your way, and whether you can transform your daily choices into lifelong habits.

This is not an ending—it is your evolution.

⚔ *You have fought the battle within yourself. Now, you are ready to build something greater.*

Prepare for Season Two. Your mission is clear. The legacy begins now.

COMING NEXT:

Book Two–Season of Integration